Backyard Pioneers

the neighborhood naturalist

Story Quest Walks

By

MENTOR AGILITY

ISBN: 979-8-9853539-5-2

Illustration and Design by Kevin Gleason

Printed in the United States of America

www.MentorAgility.com

Mentor Agility LLC
Jackson Hole, WY 83001

Contents

Letter to Parents

Think back upon your most vivid childhood memories. Think of how you used to play and when you felt the most alive. These memories probably involve outdoor places. After all, for most of us, the times when we feel most free, present, whole and connected are the times when we find ourselves in a spectacular natural setting. Perhaps you have memories of playing hide-and-seek in a wilderness space or vacant lot down the street from your home, hiking the local trails with your family or sitting around a glowing campfire watching the setting sun color the horizon?

Maybe it is the ancient timelessness of these activities that stirs our spirit. Perhaps it is the way our responsibilities and obligations are put into perspective by a sky full of stars. It is the comfort we find in remembering that everything we need comes from the earth, and that makes us feel content in nature.

As parents, we know that it is essential to the health and happiness of our children to have an intimate connection with nature. Indeed, it is essential to the health and happiness of the planet as a whole for our kids to understand the vital connections between the natural world and our lives. The intention of this book is to give you and your children adventurous activities that will take you outdoors to explore the earth under your feet. Essentially, these are introductory ecology lessons. They will put your family on the path to becoming more active, conscious participants in your ecosystem. We hope they will inspire further exploration into the names, habits and needs of the wild birds, plants and animals who share your world with you. This book is a tool to help you and your children rediscover the fascinating beauty, interdependence and design of the natural world, both around you and within you.

In a time when kids are learning more about nature from looking at a screen than they are from directly experiencing it firsthand, we hope to give you the tools to introduce them to a more sustainable, intricate, and beautiful source of stimulation for their curiosity. These activities are designed to be adaptable to any ecological region. They can be experienced in a million different ways depending upon your geography, season, weather, local wildlife, city size and mood. It is important to remember that these lessons are only words upon a page. Their richness can only be appreciated when you and your children bring them to life in your own backyard wilderness.

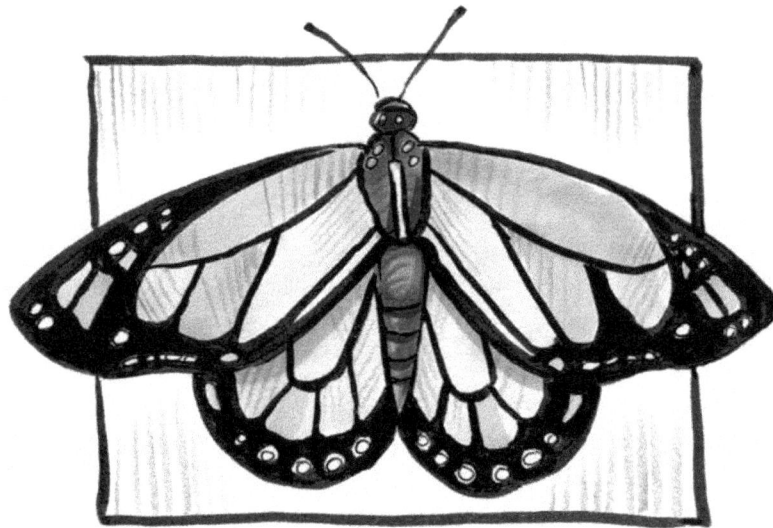

Monarch Butterfly • Danaus plexippus

Letter to Students

Now don't get me wrong … computers, televisions, iPods and cell phones are fascinating objects that have the ability to make the world a smaller place. After all, I am sitting before one right now, sharing these ideas with you at the touch of a button. These tools and toys are helping your generation become the most educated generation ever. But, at the same time, they are hiding beautiful things from our eyes. We are using our five senses less and being distracted from a much bigger world outside of the screen.

This is a book about the types of things that a person could never learn from a computer. The detail of what this book is going to point to could never be measured in gigabytes. The beauty could never be shown on even the most high-tech screen. You will only understand the beauty and complexity of what we are describing when you see it for yourself.

This is a book to get you and your parents outdoors and away from the busy lives you all lead. Your goal is to take your parents out into the wild parts of your neighborhood and to get them to play again. You will do experiments, go on scavenger hunts, stumble around blindfolded, and get down on your hands and knees to study insects. Your parents will, too. The big question is, who will learn the most, you or them? Remember that the activities are just part of what you want to be doing when you go exploring outside. Once there, nature might lead you to look in other more fascinating directions. Show your parents how to play and have an adventurous spirit. We hope you have a great time. We hope you and your parents will laugh together often. We hope you will help each other learn to see the cycles and rhythms of the world around you.

Loving the Weeds

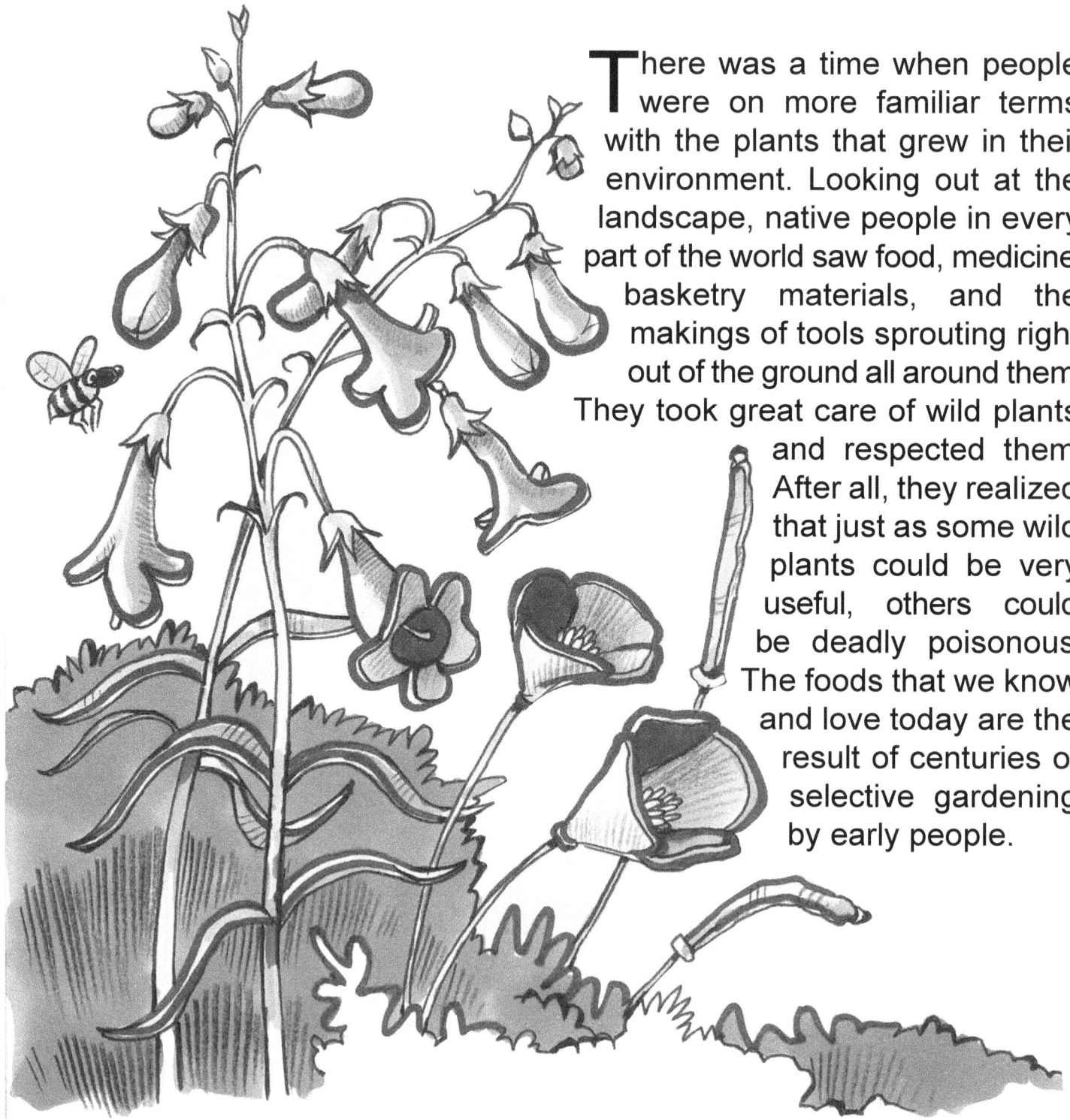

There was a time when people were on more familiar terms with the plants that grew in their environment. Looking out at the landscape, native people in every part of the world saw food, medicine, basketry materials, and the makings of tools sprouting right out of the ground all around them. They took great care of wild plants and respected them. After all, they realized that just as some wild plants could be very useful, others could be deadly poisonous. The foods that we know and love today are the result of centuries of selective gardening by early people.

1

This is a collection of lessons to get you on the path to learning about the plants that share your environment. You will be challenged to explore herbs and plants from your garden and ecosystem, using your five senses. You will try to intuit and then research the edible, medicinal, and other uses of common herbs. You will learn about the five most common poisonous plants found in North America so that you can admire them from a distance. You will observe the ways that flowers and their pollinators have evolved to fit each other. Most importantly, you will begin to develop a growing relationship with the plants that grow and change each year in your environment.

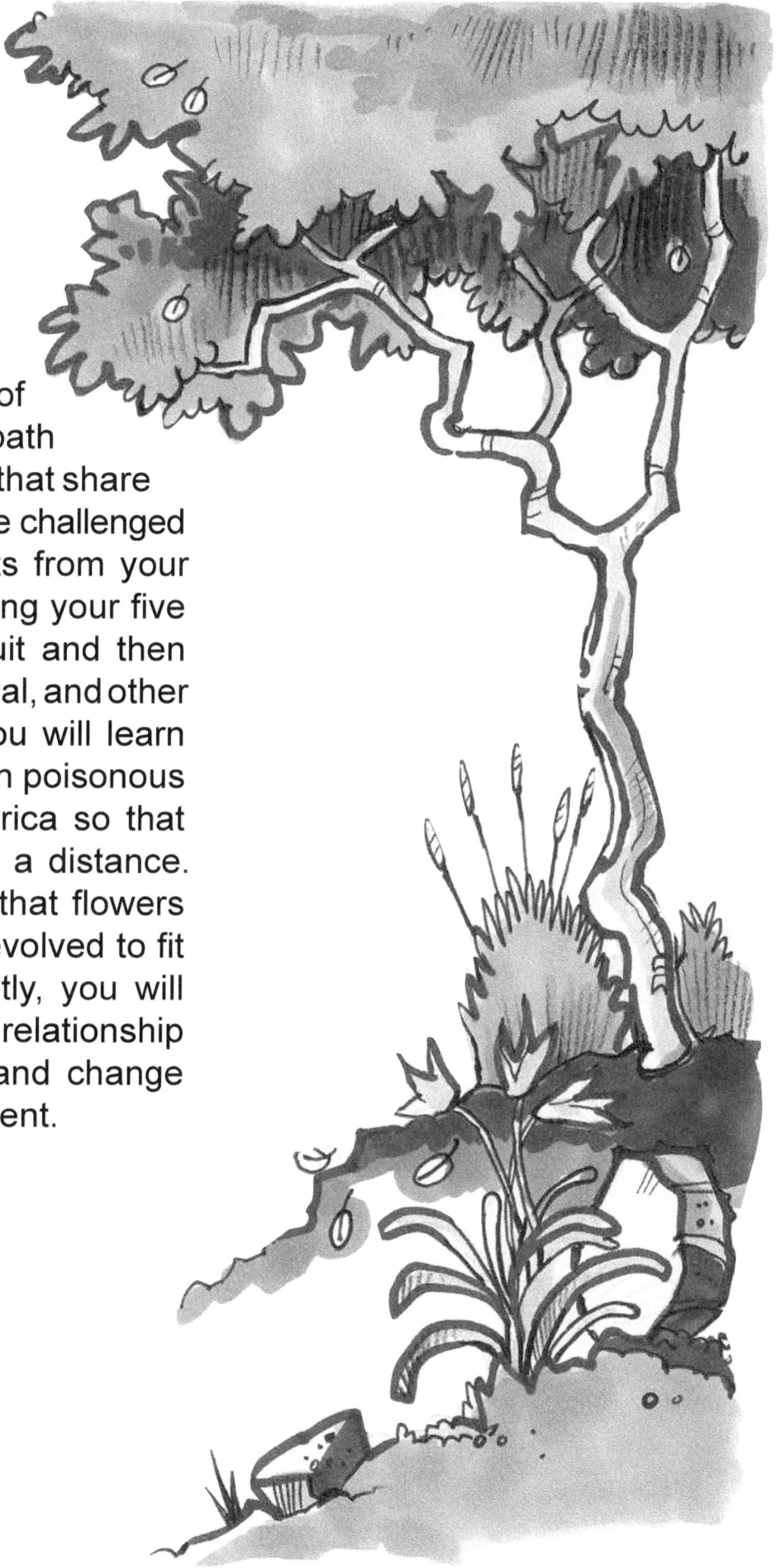

Sense Safaris: Scent Safari

Background: Discover your backyard by using all of your senses. You will appreciate your backyard in unique ways after this investigation.

Directions:

- Partner with a parent to collect six plants from the garden. Caution: Do not collect poisonous plants!
- Identify each plant, or give it your own descriptive name.
- Number your plants.
- Starting with plant #1, close your eyes and deeply inhale its scent.
- Commit that scent, the plant's name and its number to your memory.
- Continue to smell all of your plants using the same technique. Next, have your parent randomly hand you one of the six plants for you to identify with your eyes closed.
- Open your eyes and check to see if you are correct.
- Keep track of your successes.

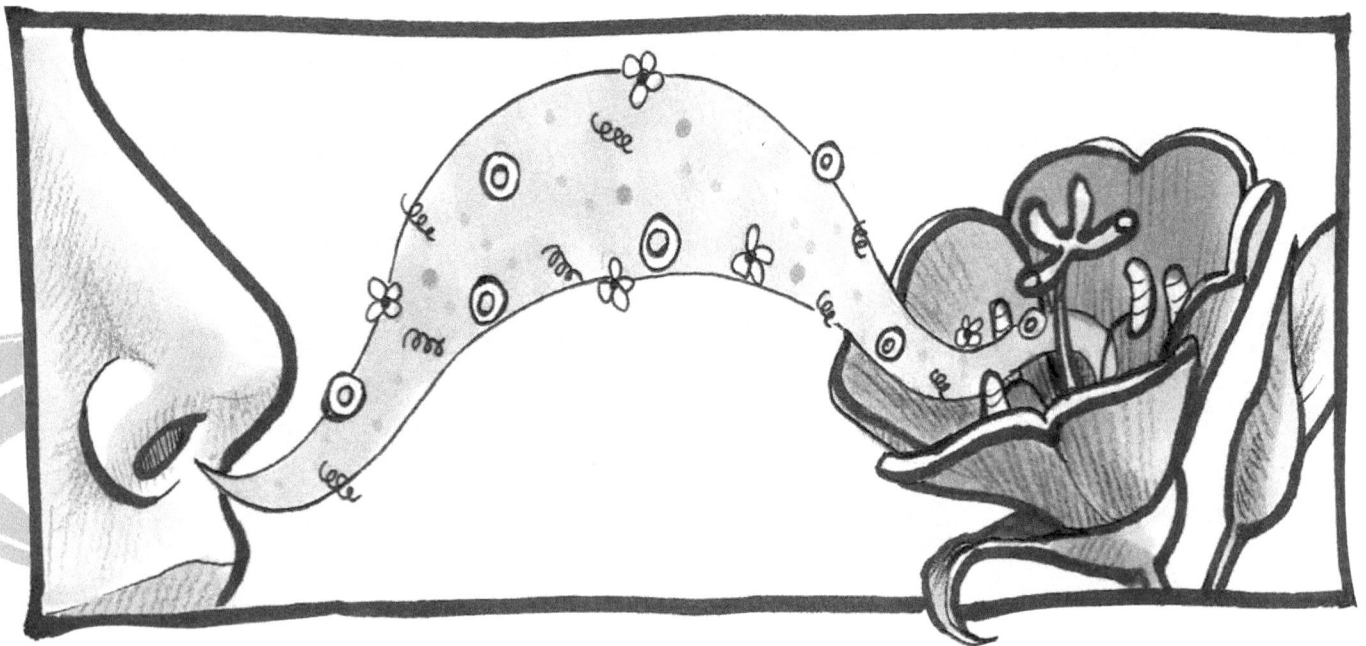

Plant # and Name	Successfully ID'd 1st time	Successfully ID'd 2nd time	Successfully ID'd 3rd time
1.			
2.			
3.			

Plant # and Name	Successfully ID'd 1st time	Successfully ID'd 2nd time	Successfully ID'd 3rd time
4.			
5.			
6.			

Challenge: Switch roles and have your parent identify the scents. Who has the better scent memory?

Sense Safaris: Taste Safari

Background: Discover your backyard by using all of your senses. You will appreciate your backyard in unique ways after this investigation.

Directions: Collect five fresh edible herbs from your yard, a local farm stand, or grocery store. Complete the following herb chart:

Herb Name	Sketch	Description of Taste	Do you like it?	What are its uses?
1.				
2.				
3.				
4.				
5.				

Challenge: While blindfolded, see if you can identify herbs by tasting them. Challenge a friend or a parent to an herb-tasting identification contest!

square stems

toothed leaves

bugs like it, too

Spearmint is named for its spear-shaped leaves, which have a very distinct smell when you crush them. The aroma is somehow both sweet and spicy, reminding one of toothpaste or chewing gum. Mint has been used to freshen breath for centuries because it has antibacterial properties and smells clean. Spearmint flavor is cool, crisp and refreshing. It is often used in summer salads like tabouleh to help cool people down. Warm, steamy spearmint tea can help soothe an upset stomach.

Spearmint · Mentha spicata

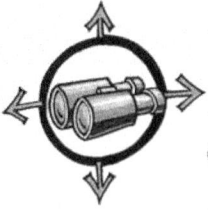 *observation*

Sense Safaris: Sight Safari

Background: Discover your backyard by using all of your senses. You will appreciate your backyard in unique ways after this investigation.

Directions: Locate your favorite plant in a garden, local park, or florist shop. Name the plant and then sketch it here in full color. Then, answer the questions on the following page.

Plant's Name:_____

Use your imagination to answer the following questions:

⊮ Why did you choose this particular plant?

_____

_____

_____

_____

⊮ Is it the shape, color, texture or size of the plant that appeals to you? Explain.

_____

_____

_____

⊮ If the plant could come alive, what would it sound like and how would it act?
Would it be a friend or foe to man? Explain.

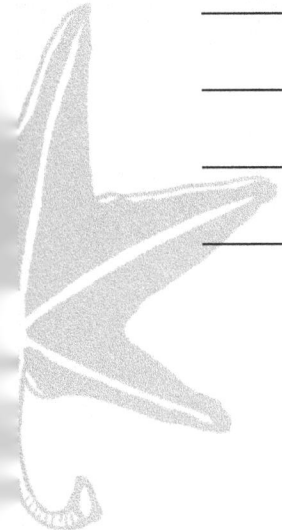

_____

_____

_____

_____

_____

_____

_____

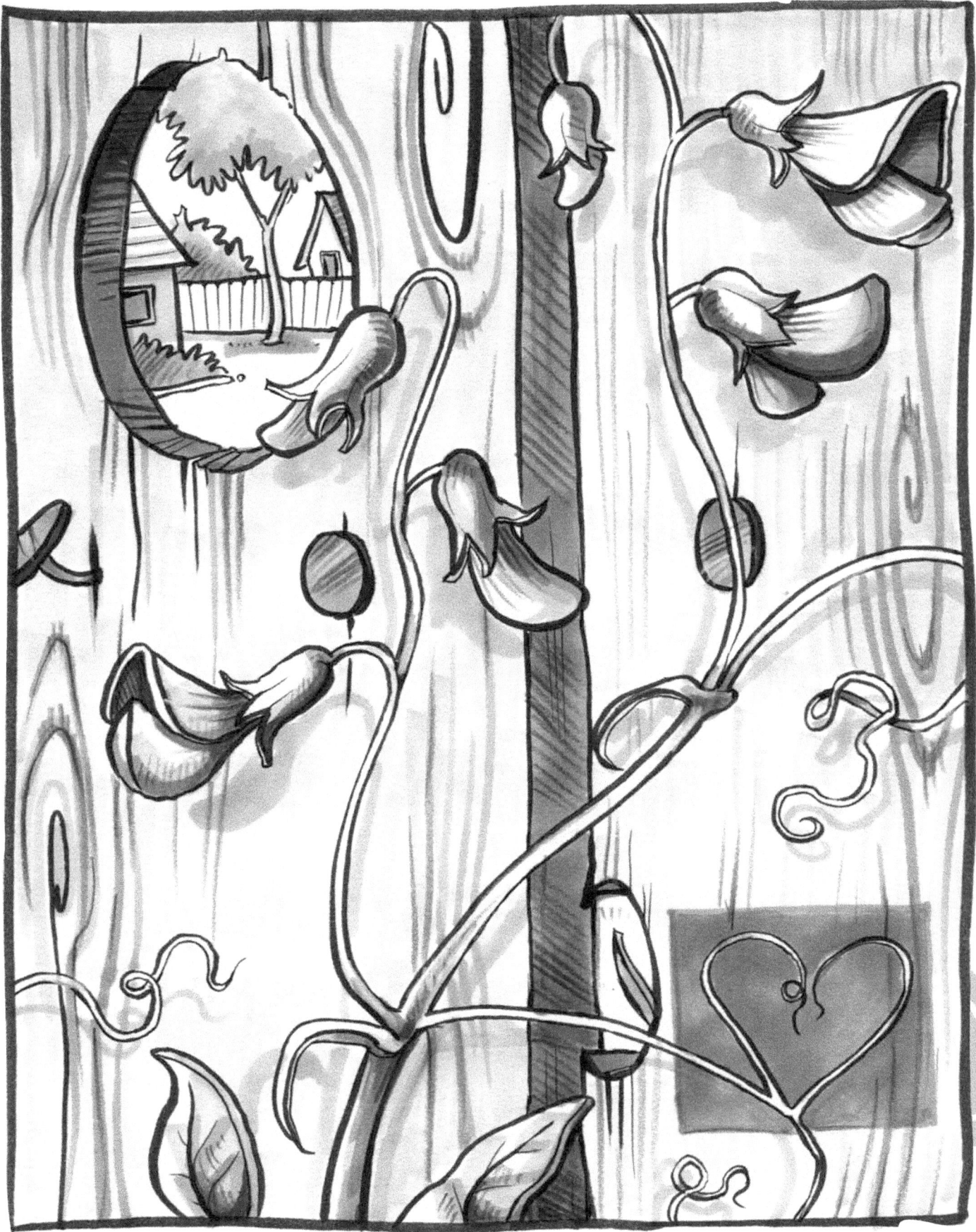

Over the next several weeks, draw your plant and try to record its changes through the seasons. What insects seem to visit it and what does it offer them? What do its flowers look like, and how do the seeds form?

It can be fascinating to realize the changes that a single plant goes through and then look outdoors and realize that every weed and tree goes through its own cycles.

Flower Power

Background: The color, size, shape and scent of a flower all serve a purpose for the pollination process.

Directions: Observe pollinators in the garden. Record the type, color, size and scent of the flower visited by the pollinator. Review your data and generalize what kinds of flowers attract specific pollinators.

Pollinator	Flower Characteristics	Size (sm,med,large)	Scent
Bee			
Generalizations about bees:			
Butterfly			
Generalizations about butterflies:			
Hummingbird			
Generalizations about hummingbirds:			

Pollinator	Flower Characteristics	Size (sm,med,large)	Scent
Moth			
Generalizations about moths:			
Beetle			
Generalizations about beetles:			
Bat			
Generalizations about bats:			

humming bird sage · salvia spathacea

How do you think hummingbird sage (see drawing) gets its name? Who benefits most from this design: the plant or the hummingbird? Which do you think came first?

Im"pressed" by Flowers

Background: Use this tested method to preserve your colorful and beautiful flowers indefinitely. Thinner flowers and foliage work the best.

Directions: Pick a variety of fresh flowers and foliage. Place the flowers flat on a piece of wax paper and cover with a second piece of wax paper. Slip the sandwiched flowers into an old encyclopedia or other thick book. Weigh down the book with other books, and in two weeks, you will have pressed plants.

On the next page, create a picture or design with your pressed plant parts. Give your creation a title. (See the example below.)

Pressed Flower Design

Title:_____

Stay Away!
Keep the Hives at Bay!

Background: To itch or not to itch? That is the question! Everyone in North America should learn to recognize the BIG FIVE poisonous plants that invade the country from the East Coast to the West Coast. From mildly irritating to deadly, these plants will not harm anyone if they can be recognized and avoided.

Big Five
Poisonous Plants:

- Poison Oak (pictured below)
- Poison Ivy
- Poison Sumac
- Poison Hemlock
- Castor Bean

Directions: Using the Internet or a local plant field guide, find images of these plants. Research which ones you are most likely to encounter in your region and what their most recognizable characteristics are. Remember that the leaves do not always look green and shiny. Each of these plants looks different depending upon the time of year. Make sketches with notes that will help you remember how to identify them when you see them in real life. Now, see if you can find one of these plants, or other toxic plants, as you are out wandering around. It gives us confidence to know them and to learn the role they play in the ecosystem.

Name of Plant: _____

ϒ   Places it is likely to be found: _____

ϒ   Distinguishing characteristics: _____

_____

ϒ   What is poisonous about it? _____

Sketch it here:

Although poison oak can be a pest for hikers, birds love the small berries that it produces in the spring. It is interesting to see that what is poisonous for one animal is not necessarily harmful for others. Poison oak provides shelter for small animals and the red leaves can be beautiful in the fall. Just don't touch it or you'll itch for days.

 *activity*

Needle Naming

Background: You can easily identify most evergreen trees by using this simple key.

Directions: Become a modern-day David Douglas and collect needles from trees in your area. Sketch them and then identify them as Pine, Fir, or Spruce needles. Use this quick guide to identify trees with needles.

1. Needles fastened together in bundles of two to three...............................Pine

2. Needles all separate, attached individually to the branch:

    a.   Flat to the touch...Fir

    b.   Square and easily rolled between fingers.............................Spruce

Specimen #1

ID: _____

Specimen #2

ID: _____

Specimen #3

ID: _____

Specimen #4

ID: _____

Focus on: David Douglas

David Douglas loved plants. At the age of eleven, this Scotsman quit his formal education and became a gardener's apprentice. After seven years, he was eager to learn more about plants, so he enrolled in college. His professors were very impressed with his enthusiasm and knowledge.

In 1824, he was chosen to travel to the Pacific Northwest in America to collect plants for Great Britain. There he studied, named and collected 240 species of plants, including the Douglas-Fir, Ponderosa Pine, California Poppy, and the Lodgepole Pine. He changed the gardens and forests of England with the introduction of these plants.

Sadly, David Douglas died at the age of 35 when he fell into a pit trap in the Hawaii

Islands. He was apparently crushed by a bull that had also fallen into the trap. This was a tragic end for this brilliant botanist. However, David Douglas lives on in the hundreds of Western plants he introduced to the world.

Be a frontier explorer: David Douglas was responsible for discovering and naming many trees in America. If you were to rename your favorite tree, what would it be? Explain:

_____

_____

_____

_____

_____

_____

_____

_____

_____

 *concerned citizen*

Predator Hunt

Background: In this lesson, you will discover the predatory insects that are hunting amongst the flowers and bushes in your yard or the wild spaces near your home. You will learn about their roles in keeping plant-eating bugs in check. You will understand why spraying pesticides on plants might not be the best way to control plant-eating bugs.

Think about this: Take a moment to consider herbivorous (plant-eating) and carnivorous (meat-eating) animals that are native to the region where you live. In some regions, an example of these might be ground squirrels and red-tailed hawks. Squirrels, like most herbivores, have many offspring. These young squirrels reach maturity and grow very quickly because they eat acorns, roots and plants, which are literally all around them. Hawks, on the other hand, like most predators, have relatively few offspring. These young birds take longer to reach maturity because they need to be taught special skills in order to catch their dinners. There are many more herbivores in an environment than carnivores, usually a ratio of about 10:1. This is because it takes several squirrels a week to feed a hungry hawk.

assassin bug

aphid
(lunch)

Directions: Go outside on a predatory insect hunt. Take a magnifying glass with you if you would like. You might consider starting by looking for plants that look as if bugs have been eating part of their leaves. There you will most likely find herbivorous bugs, if you look closely. Where you find these bugs, you will probably also find carnivores. Common carnivorous bugs include ladybugs, lacewings, praying mantises, and spiders.

Keep a tally of how many herbivores and how many carnivores you find, and make a small sketch of insects that you aren't sure of. Do you see other creatures eating bugs as well, such as lizards or birds? Then answer the questions on the following page.

Insect Name (If you don't know it, make one up.)	Sketch and Notes	Carnivore or Herbivore?	What is it eating?

Concerned Citizen: Imagine that you were to spray pesticides in the garden and kill most of the herbivores and predators on the plants.

❧ With the first spray, which population would lose more members? _____

_____

❧ Who would repopulate the most quickly, herbivores or predators? Think about the numbers of offspring they typically have and the time it takes to reach maturity.

_____

❧ What effect will this have on the garden? What will happen if the gardener sprays again?

_____

_____

_____

*F*ood for Thought: Understanding the importance of insects in pollinating our food and keeping each other in check leads many people to buy organic produce. Try to think about other reasons it might be a good idea to buy vegetables that aren't sprayed with pesticides. In the space to the right, design a public awareness poster that helps others to see the benefits of sharing some of our lettuce with the bugs.

ladybeetle

lacewing

Winged Travelers

2

What are birds singing about as the sun glows warm over the horizon each morning? Birdsong can lift our spirits and wake us from our daydreams. Developing an awareness of birds and their behaviors can help us to become more in tune with our environments. We learn to see their connection to the changing seasons and the plants around us. For example, when the first elderberries begin to ripen in spring, we know it will be just days before the red finches arrive.

Many of us admire the incredible freedom of birds. These winged travelers soar through the sky on seasonal migrations to exotic places, stopping for short spells in our backyards. What do birds see on their journeys that take them north and south through the seasons? In the following lessons, you will experiment with attracting birds to your yard and identifying them. You will research the diverse characteristics of birds that allow them to live in the various climates in the world. And, using technology, you will try to get a bird's-eye view of your own neighborhood.

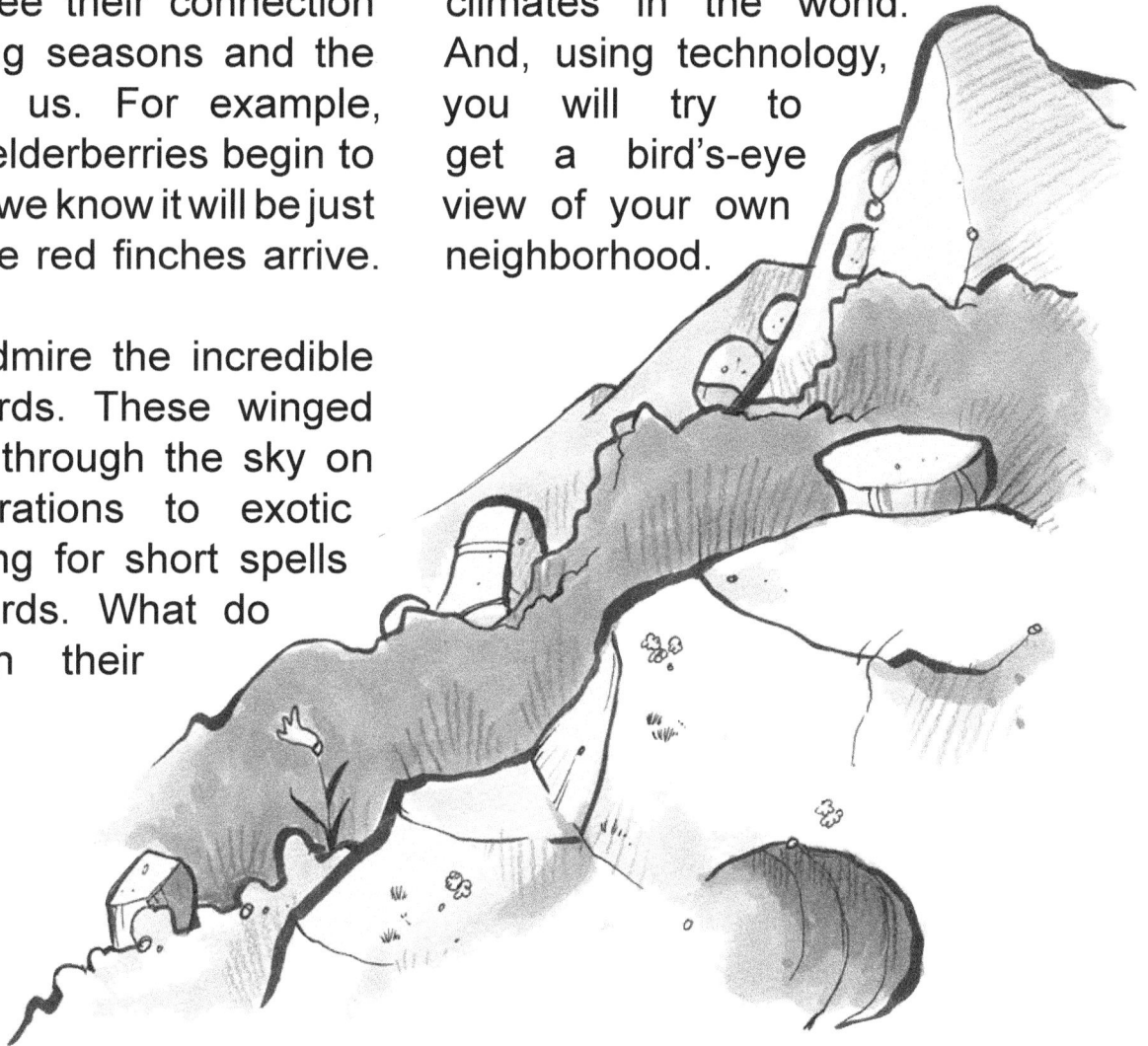

Adopt a Tree

Background: Large trees are the treasure of our Earth. They provide homes and food for animals, shade for plants, and oxygen for us.

Directions: Find a large tree and adopt it. Take a photograph of the tree during the four different seasons, and observe it carefully. Be sure to take your pictures from exactly the same spot each time.

Materials: digital camera, tree identification book

Hypothesis: Explain some of the changes you expect to see during the different seasons.

_____

_____

_____

_____

_____

Spring Observations

❧ Type of tree:_____

❧ Description of tree: _____

❧ Birds in tree: _____

❧ Insects in tree: _____

❧ Mammals in or around tree: _____

❧ How is this tree affecting its environment? _____

Coast Live Oak · Quercus agrifolia

Summer Observations

❧ Type of tree:_____

❧ Description of tree: _____

❧ Birds in tree: _____

❧ Insects in tree: _____

❧ Mammals in or around tree: _____

❧ How is this tree affecting its environment? _____

Autumn Observations

❧ Type of tree:_____

❧ Description of tree: _____

❧ Birds in tree: _____

❧ Insects in tree: _____

❧ Mammals in or around tree: _____

❧ How is this tree affecting its environment? _____

Winter Observations

❧ Type of tree:_____

❧ Description of tree: _____

❧ Birds in tree: _____

❧ Insects in tree: _____

❧ Mammals in or around tree: _____

❧ How is this tree affecting its environment? _____

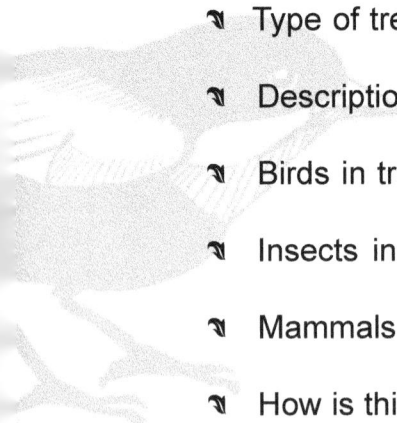

Spring Sketch

Summer Sketch

Autumn Sketch

Winter Sketch

Bird Banquet

Background: Investigate bird feeding behaviors by doing this delicious experiment. Licking is permitted!

Directions: Find three pinecones of the same size and do the following:.

To Pinecone #1:
- Attach a thin wire so pinecone can be placed in a tree.

To Pinecone #2:
- Attach a thin wire so pinecone can be placed in a tree.
- Melt in a pan 3 tbsp. peanut butter + 2 tbsp. shortening. Spread on cone.

To Pinecone #3
- Attach a thin wire so pinecone can be placed in a tree.
- Melt in a pan 3 tbsp. peanut butter + 2 tbsp. shortening. Spread on cone.
- Press 2 tbsp. of sunflower seeds into the peanut butter mixture.

Place all three pinecones in a tree at the same height above the ground.

Hypothesis: What do you think will happen? Why?

_____

_____

_____

_____

_____

Observe the pinecones from a distance. Note: You may need to wait up to a week for your "gift" to be discovered by wild creatures.

Record data in the chart to the right. Then, answer the questions on the following page.

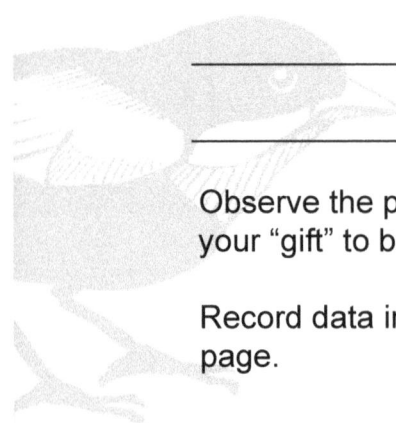

	Pinecone 1	Pinecone 2	Pinecone 3
Names of Visitors			
Number of Visitors			
Length of Stay			

Sketch one of the visitors below:

Questions:

What is the name of your visitor? _____

Which pinecone did it visit and when? _____

Which pinecone was the control (not changed)? _____

_____

Did the sunflower seeds make Pinecone #3 more attractive to the visitors?

_____

_____

Revise:

Which part of the experiment would you change if you were to do it again? _____

_____

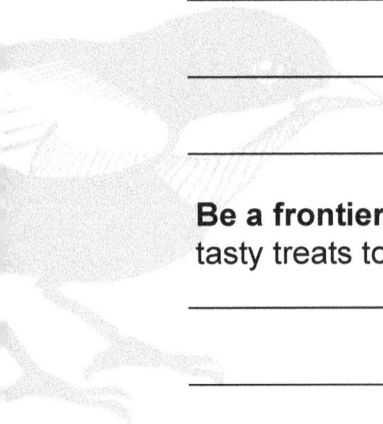

_____

_____

Be a frontier explorer: Run your own bird banquet experiment, choosing different tasty treats to offer, and record the results.

_____

_____

_____

Things That Have Wings

Background: Brainstorm organisms that have wings. Certainly, you've thought of birds. Next, you've probably thought about winged insects. Finally, you might have thought about the one flying mammal, the bat. As you can imagine, all of these wings work to give the animal the ability to fly. Wouldn't you like to fly?

Directions: Go into your backyard and look for winged organisms. Look at a variety of wing designs. Sketch them and answer these questions. If you can't find all of them, look on the Internet for examples of the ones you are missing.

Dragonfly • *Anax junius*

Sketch a Butterfly Wing

Sketch a Dragonfly Wing

Sketch a Bird Wing

Sketch a Bat Wing

Questions:

☜ What do all of the wings have in common? _____

☜ How are they different? _____

_____

☜ If you dissected each wing, which ones would be most alike? _____

_____

_____

Extension: There are fish that are called flying fish. They literally glide over the ocean waves flapping their fins vigorously. They even land on the decks of boats crossing the sea. Can you find pictures of these fish on the Internet, and discover how it is they "fly"? Are their fins really wings? Why, or why not?

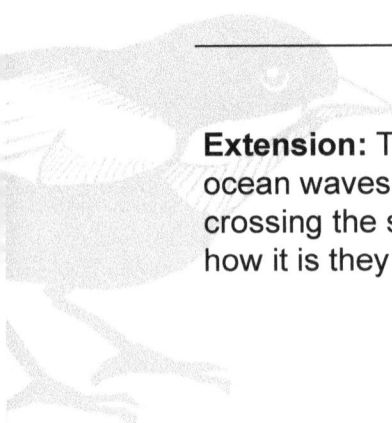

Introduction to Bird Watching

Background: One of the important skills of a bird watcher is learning to identify a bird they see in the wild by using a field guide. Birds in these guides are grouped in families. One way to determine the type of bird you are seeing is to look at the shape of its beak. Besides helping you to key the bird, this shape can tell you quite a bit about what the bird eats and what its habits are.

Instructions: With sketching supplies like colored pencils, go on a walk searching for birds. Binoculars are not essential, but they can really help you see more detail. It is probably best to go early in the morning or in the late afternoon. Try looking where there is fresh water or trees for shelter. Open your ears and think like a bird. When you find a bird who looks like it will stay around for a while, quietly creep as close as you can without frightening it away.

Draw the bird in as much detail as you can. Then, fill in the chart on the next page. Pay particular attention to its color patterns, the length of its tail, its general size, and the shape of its beak.

What would you name this bird?	What could its size be compared to?	What colors do you see in its feathers?	What does it appear to be eating?	Is it by itself or with other birds of its kind?

Reflections: Look at the beak shapes below. They are formed to perform certain activities. Think about the shape of the beak on the bird you drew. What do you suppose this bird eats? Does its body size, shape, and flying style confirm this?

_____

_____

_____

_____

_____

Further Investigation: Go to the library and check out a field guide to birds in your region. See if you can find your bird in the book. Research its nesting behaviors, migration routes and food preferences. The next time you encounter this bird, it will be like a familiar friend. See if you can learn the sound of its song so that you can know it is nearby even when you can't see it.

seed eating

pecking

insect hunting

shore probing

wood pecking

hunting

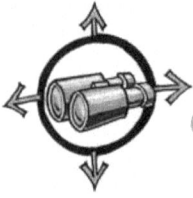

Sense Safaris: Sound Safari

Background: Discover your backyard by using all of your senses. You will appreciate your backyard in unique ways after this investigation.

Directions: Choose a safe spot outside and stand quietly with your eyes closed. Listen to the world around you. Mentally identify all the sounds you hear. Open your eyes and record the source of the sounds. Repeat this investigation at different times of the day.

Date:	Time:
Man-made sounds:	Natural sounds:
Date:	Time:
Man-made sounds:	Natural sounds:
Date:	Time:
Man-made sounds:	Natural sounds:
Date:	Time:
Man-made sounds:	Natural sounds:

Google Earth for the Birds

Background: This activity will give you a new perspective on your turf and how bird-friendly it is.

Directions:

- Find an aerial photograph of your home on Google Earth™ by typing in your address.
- Make a "bird's-eye" sketch of your home and your yard after looking at the image you find.
- Alternately, type in your school's address and make a sketch of the grounds of your school.
- Imagine that you are a specific bird flying over the area that you sketched. Which bird would you choose to be, and why?
- Find a picture of your bird on the Internet or in a North American bird book.
- Name and sketch that bird.
- Research the needs and habitat preferences of your bird.
- List and sketch what might attract you to the sketched area. Would it be the trees, bushes or food available?
- Finally, answer the questions on page 52.

Aerial Sketch of your Area

Bird's Name: _____

Bird's Habitat: _____

_____

Food: _____

_____

Behavior: _____

_____

_____

_____

Area's Attractions: _____

_____

_____

_____

_____

Area's Hazards: _____

_____

_____

_____

_____

Improvement plans to make the area more bird-friendly: _____

_____

_____

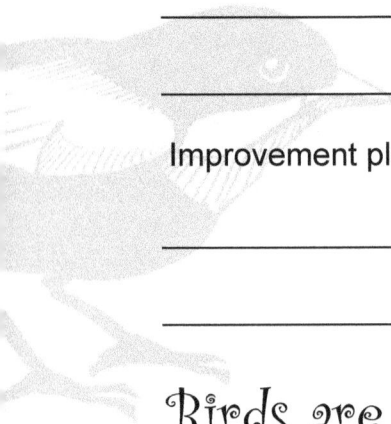

Birds are beneficial to our beautiful Earth!

activity

Bird Champions

Introduction: There are more than 10,000 species of birds in the world. With that kind of competition, you really would have to be special to distinguish yourself as a bird!

Directions: Put on your thinking cap, and match the species to the records they hold. One bird holds two of the records. *The answers are on the following page, so don't peek until you make your guesses!*

Record	Your Guesses (from the list below)
Smallest Body	
Fastest in the Air	
Fastest on Land	
Fastest Swimmer	
Longest Beak	
Longest Tongue	
Biggest Eyes	
Longest Migration	
Longest Living	
Best Hearing	
Oldest Known (extinct)	

Species Choices: *Archaeopteryx, Arctic Tern, Australian Pelican, Bee Hummingbird, Cockatoo, Flamingo, Gentoo Penguin, Great Horned Owl, Ostrich (x2), Peregrine Falcon*

Red Shouldered Hawk *Buteo lineatus*

Answers to Bird Champions Quiz:

Record	Answers (from previous page)
Smallest Body	Bee Hummingbird
Fastest in the Air	Peregrine Falcon
Fastest on Land	Ostrich
Fastest Swimmer	Gentoo Penguin
Longest Beak	Australian Pelican
Longest Tongue	Flamingo
Biggest Eyes	Ostrich
Longest Migration	Arctic Tern
Longest Living	Cockatoo
Best Hearing	Great Horned Owl
Oldest Known (extinct)	Archaeopteryx

Focus on: John James Audubon

The young Frenchman John James Audubon sailed to America to start a new life when he was just eighteen years old. He was a keen observer of nature and loved living on his family's land near Philadelphia, Pennsylvania. Audubon was curious about birds' migration patterns and decided to tie short strings to birds' legs in the fall as a way of identifying particular individuals. To his delight, many of the birds with strings on their legs returned in the spring! This experiment may have been the first banding of birds in America.

What was first a hobby became Audubon's sole profession as bird drawings became the focus of his life. Starting in the 1820s, Audubon began his quest to sketch every bird species in America. After fourteen years of travel, painting and financial struggle, Audubon completed 497 sketches of species of birds out of the roughly 700 existing American species. His paintings were praised for their life-like qualities, dra-

matic composition, and natural backgrounds. Each print measured 39 x 26 inches, and each bird was painted life-size. Audubon's insistence on painting actual size had its challenges, however, especially when he encountered the California Condor!

John James Audubon did not start the famous Audubon Society, but he inspired the society's founders. He will forever be remembered as a gifted naturalist, an avid hunter and a strong conservationist. His spectacularly beautiful prints can be found in reproductions of his book, "Birds of America."

Your Backyard Wilderness

Have you ever tried to picture what your neighborhood looked like before the roads, homes, and people were there? Perhaps it was a farm or ranch at one time. But what did it look like even before that? If you live in a big city, the town and piece of ground your home sits on has likely gone through many changes over the years. But no matter where you live, at one point it was wild land inhabited by all kinds of creatures.

Can you imagine the wilderness that existed where your neighborhood now rests? What types of plants and animals do you think made up the ecosystem? Some of those wild ones are still around.

3

Many of these creatures, such as birds, frogs, lizards or squirrels, can be seen during the day sharing our landscapes with us. Others have been pushed out of developed areas into whatever remaining wilderness they can find. Still others have learned to visit our yards only in the dark and quiet of the night.

In the following lessons, we will try to learn more about all of these creatures and study the role that mammals, amphibians, and reptiles play in an environment. We will be set on the path to recognizing the subtle signs left by the visitors that come to our yards and nearby open spaces. We begin to realize that there really is not a clear border between the human world and that of wild animals. We all share one beautiful global habitat.

Who Goes There?

Introduction: Do you ever wonder about the animals that visit your yard after dark? As you begin your inside nighttime life, many nocturnal animals begin their activities in your yard. In this activity you will get some ideas about how you can record their visits without becoming a nocturnal explorer yourself.

Directions: There are a few methods for recording tracks. Choose the one that best suits your environment.

Method 1: In an area where animals are likely to travel — opening of a gate, edge of a pond, near a large tree — place a two-foot square patch of damp, fine sand, about two inches thick. Be sure to check for footprints early each morning. This method is great for collecting footprints of mammals and birds.

Method 2: In an area where insects might be scurrying about — near a woodpile, close to a pond, in the garden — place a small ceramic plate. The plate should be an old one that you no longer use. Coat the plate's top with a layer of carbon by holding the flame of a candle next to the surface of the plate. Move the flame around to avoid overheating the plate. This procedure should be supervised by an adult. In the morning, look carefully for trails left behind by busy insects. As a bonus, you might want to bait the plate with a bit of honey in the center.

Method 3: If your soil has a high clay content, you can use a layer of mud to record night visitors. Substitute firm mud for the sand in Method 1.

Record every track with a digital camera. Print the photos and try to identify the tracks. Use a search engine to locate the tracks on the Internet, or buy a tracking book with life-size pictures of tracks. Think like an explorer, be patient, and have fun!

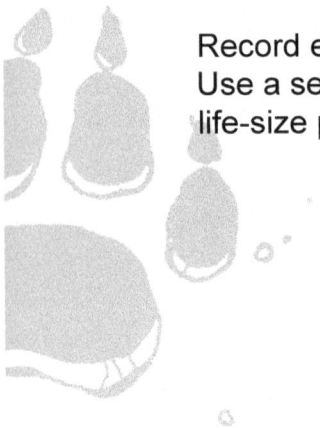

*E*xperienced trackers can tell how old tracks are just by looking at them. How do you think they might do this? Often you will see the tracks of a predator following behind the tracks of a prey. Can you guess who made these tracks? The common backyard bandit can be found sneaking up on you on the next page.

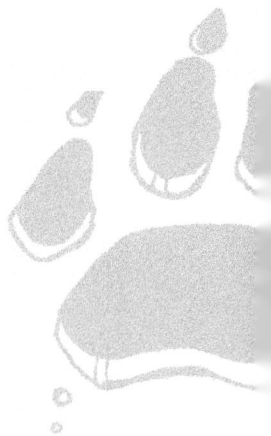

Backyard Pioneers

activity

Quiet as a Creature

Background: Many animals have perfected the ability to hunt almost silently. In this activity, you will think and act like an animal. Invite five or more friends to do this activity with you. It's a "blast!"

Directions:

- Find two spray bottles and fill them with water.

- Have your friends form a circle about 20 feet in diameter.

- Place two people in the center, seated back to back.

- Blindfold both people and hand them the spray bottles.

- Tell the center people to spray in the direction of any sound of an approaching person.

- Have the people on the outside take turns trying to sneak up on the blindfolded people and tap them without being squirted with water.

- If a person is successful in creeping up on a middle person, she takes that person's place.

- If she is not successful, she returns to the outside and another person attempts to creep up on the center people.

- You might want to take off your shoes!

Good luck!

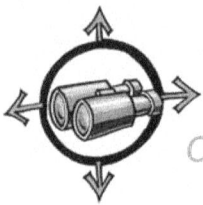

Eating Sunlight

Background: When you really sit down to think about it, everything on this planet eats sunlight. Carnivores eat herbivores. Herbivores eat plants. Plants, through photosynthesis, convert sunlight, water and carbon dioxide into sugars called carbohydrates. This solar energy is the original source of the calories that are passed through the food chain to us.

Think about this: The next time you eat lunch, try to see if you can imagine the plants and sunlight that were at the root of all the ingredients in your meal.

Directions: In this activity, you will be challenged to go outside and make a list of all the wild plants, insects, animals, birds and other creatures that you can find in your neighborhood. The longer the list is, the better. You don't have to find them all today to include them on your list. For example, if you have seen raccoon tracks in your yard before, you can include them.

For each organism on your list, try to think of all the other things on the list that you believe it might eat and all of the things that might eat it. After you have filled in the chart, make the longest food chain you can, starting with sunlight on one end of the paper and the highest predator you can think of on the opposite side.

To consider: What eats this highest predator? You might have to think about what happens after it dies. How are animals returned to the earth? When they reach this part of the food chain and are returned to soil, who uses them next? Could the food chain be considered a cycle?

Organism List	What on the list does it eat?	What eats it?
Example: Skunk	*Snails, moss, walnuts, dandelions*	*Owls*

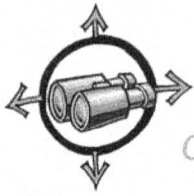

Organism Olympics

Background: The summer and winter Olympic Games collect outstanding athletes from all around the world to compete for bragging rights about who is the best in their sports. Turn the entire animal world into an Olympic contest as you do this investigation.

Directions: Imagine that all the plants and animals in your yard or neighborhood park are competing in the Organism Olympics. Here are the categories; you name the winners!

Best Flyer (more than 6 ounces): _____

Best Flyer (under 6 ounces): _____

Best Camouflaged: _____

Best Long Jumper: _____

Best Biter: _____

Best Good-Smelling: _____

Best Yucky-Smelling: _____

Best Eye Color: _____

Best Hunter: _____

Best Vision: _____

Best Climber: _____

Best Iridescence: _____

Best All-Around Athlete: _____

exhibition sport:
weight-lifting tight-rope walk

Animal Lifetimes

Background: Have you ever wondered how long certain animals live naturally? Maybe you've had a pet that has died and you wish it could have lived forever. Like people, animals have natural life spans.

Directions: This activity involves looking at a chart of animal life expectancies and challenging yourself to display the information from the chart below in a bar graph. Have fun drawing a bar graph by decorating it with pictures, footprints, or other symbols. You can use the box to the right, or alternatively, draw the graph in Word, Pages or Numbers and improve your computer skills.

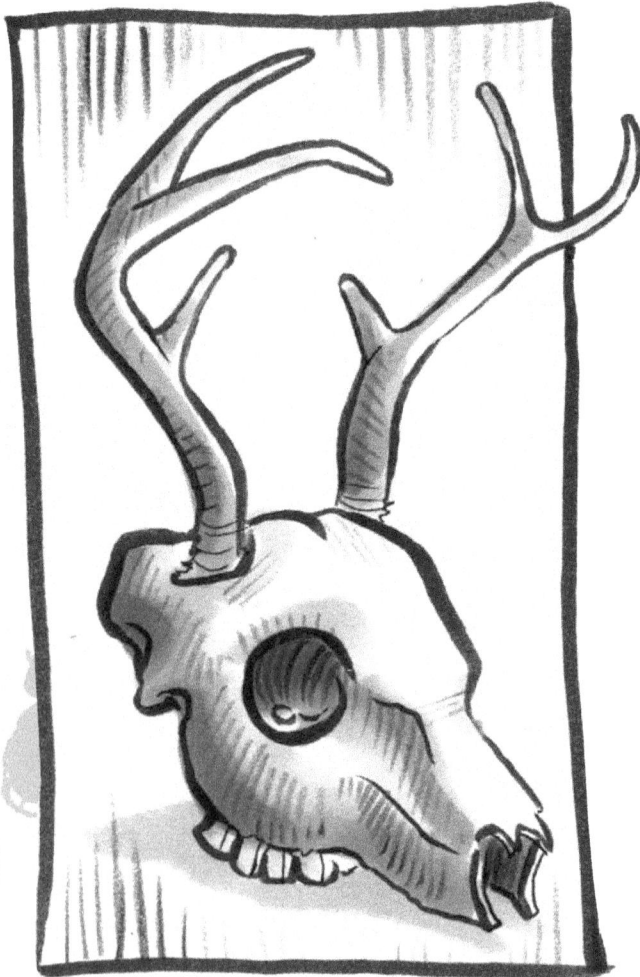

deer

Animal Name	Average Life Span (Years)
Hummingbird	5
Raccoon	10
Opossum	1.5
Squirrel	8
Black Bear	18
Coyote	6
Dog	10
Ant (Queen)	3

squirrel

blue jay

Focus on: Cats

Background: Domestic cats are important pets to many families in the United States. This activity challenges you to think about cats as exotic, domesticated animals and therefore, extensions of the human world instead of as natural, wild organisms.

Directions: Think about, and then answer, the following questions. Talk these ideas over with your family, friends and teachers. Actual statistics are upside down on the next page.

1. Do you know the approximate number of pet cats living in the USA?

Guess: _____

2. Do you know the approximate number of stray cats living in the USA?

Guess: _____

3. Do you know the approximate number of birds killed by cats each year?

Guess: _____

4. What are some great things about cats?

Response: _____

_____

_____

5. What are some negative things about cats?

Response: _____

_____

_____

6. How can a person become a responsible pet cat owner?

Response: _____

_____

_____

_____

_____

Answer Key:
1. 90 million cats
2. more than 1 million stray cats
3. more than 100,000,000 birds
4. Cats are affectionate
   Cats are good companions
   Cats are beautiful
   Cats are fun to watch
5. Cats are not a natural part of the ecosystem
   Cats are not native to the USA (ancestors from Europe and Africa)
   Cats compete with native predators
   Cats transmit diseases to native mammals
   Cats kill millions of native birds and mammals
6. Keep the cat inside
   If the cat is outside, have it on a leash
   Spay and neuter your cat
   Keep your cat healthy and well-fed
   Get the proper vaccinations for your pet cat
   Dispose of cat feces properly

Community Action!
Make a flyer in Word or Pages that tells your neighbors about responsible cat owner-ship. Post the flyers in your neighborhood to educate fellow citizens.

Alert: The American Bird Conservancy (ABC) started a national campaign called Cats Indoors! Check out the Web site for more information: www.abcbirds.org/cats

Focus on: Lewis and Clark

Captains Meriwether Lewis and William Clark led the first American overland expedition to the Pacific Coast, returning safely to their native Virginia. Their famous expedition lasted from 1803-1806. President Jefferson enthusiastically supported this exploratory trip and convinced Congress to fund it for $2,500. What a deal!

Lewis and Clark's mission was to study Indian tribes, botany, geology, wildlife and geography. In their journals they observed and described 178 different plants and 122 species and subspecies of animals. Some of the mammals they discovered were the swift fox, grizzly bear and white-tailed jackrabbit. Some of the birds they discovered included the Black-Billed Magpie, Clark's Nutcracker, and Lewis's Woodpecker.

By all accounts, the expedition of Lewis and Clark was a stunning success. Their careful observations and organized recordings of data in journals greatly increased our knowledge of the American West. Amazingly enough, only one member of their exploratory party died during their perilous trip. Doctors today believe that Sergeant Charles Floyd probably died due to a ruptured appendix.

The Neighborhood Frontier

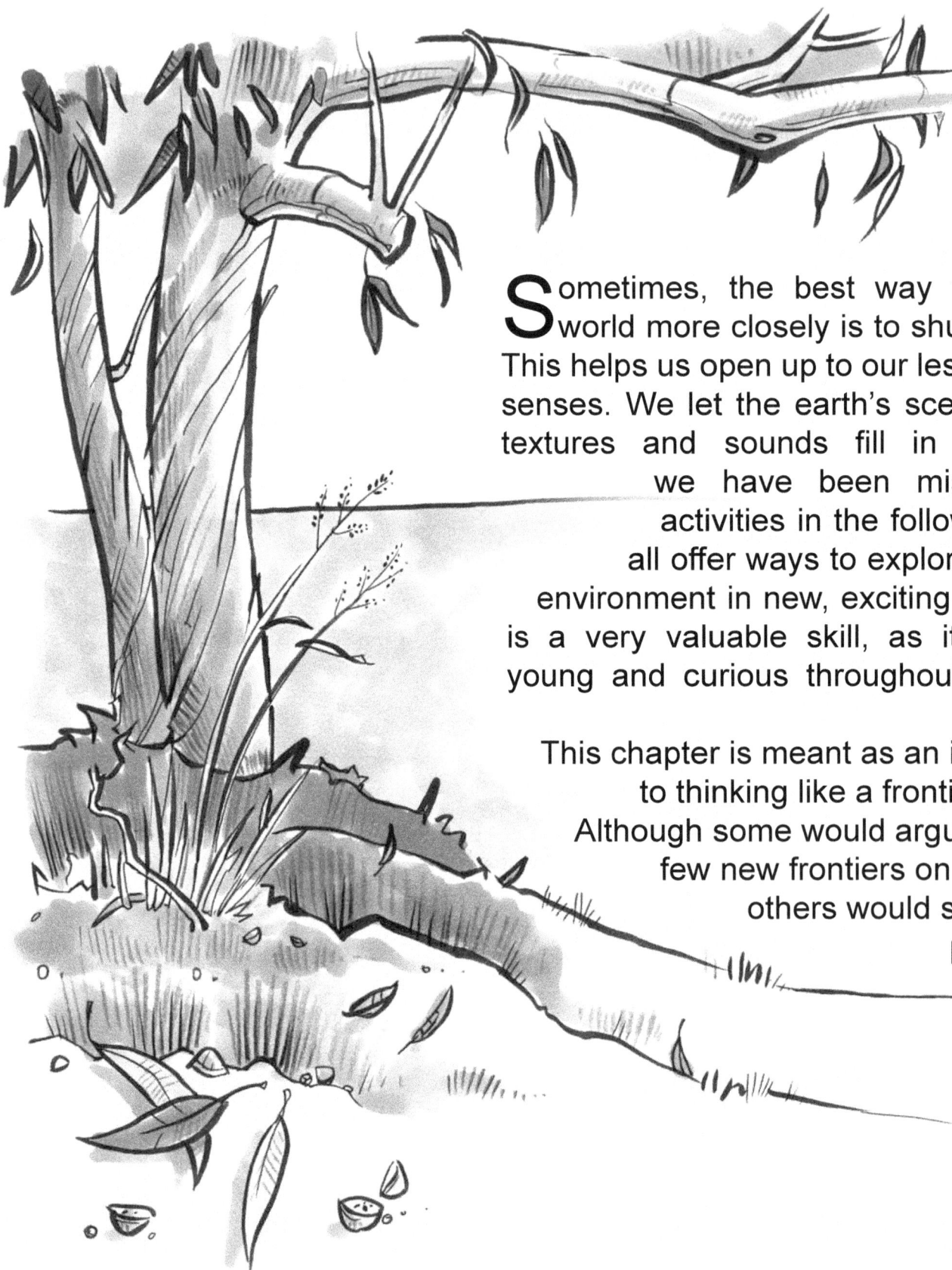

Sometimes, the best way to see the world more closely is to shut our eyes. This helps us open up to our less dominant senses. We let the earth's scents, tastes, textures and sounds fill in the areas we have been missing. The activities in the following pages all offer ways to explore a familiar environment in new, exciting ways. This is a very valuable skill, as it keeps us young and curious throughout our lives.

This chapter is meant as an introduction to thinking like a frontier explorer. Although some would argue there are few new frontiers on this planet, others would suggest that perhaps we haven't looked as deeply as we could at those we have already walked across. We are going to practice seeing the everyday plants in your garden as though they were rare, never-before-seen specimens, and smell them as though it was the first time. We will hunt for insects and sing to birds as though they could understand us. We will climb out of the ruts of our routines and habits and follow new paths and long-cuts to wherever we happen to be going. These are skills that awaken us and help us to learn and grow. We have the ability to appreciate each moment as though it were a new adventure.

Focus on: John Charles Fremont

John Charles Fremont was a military man, an explorer and a politician. Between 1842 and 1846, he explored, surveyed and mapped extensive areas from the Missouri River to the north and from the Mississippi River to the west. He is known as "The Great Pathfinder" as he mapped what was to become the Oregon Trail. His reports of the West were relayed to the U.S. government and then to the general public. He helped to encourage the great movement westward.

Historically the Fremont name is remembered throughout the West. His surname can be found as names of streets, bridges, schools, rivers and peaks, as well as four counties.

Later in life, this explorer became an important politician. He helped California become an independent state. He unsuccessfully ran for president of the United States on an anti-slavery platform. John Charles Fremont helped others discover Frontier America.

 *activity*

An Explorer's Micro-Hike Journal

Background: This activity concentrates on the micro world. Imagine that you are an insect going on a hike. What obstacles would you encounter?

Directions:

◄ Take a three-foot-long stick and place it on the ground in a natural area, avoiding cement or asphalt surfaces.

◄ Take a visual "Micro-Hike" around the stick.

◄ Using your eyes, nose, fingers and, optionally, a magnifying glass, look at a four-inch area on either side of your stick, which is about the distance between your thumb and forefinger.

◄ Dig into the ground if you want to see more.

◄ Imagine that you are an explorer like David Douglas or Lewis and Clark and that you are one of the first humans ever to see these natural objects.

◄ Be sure to describe them in detail to your friends and family back home.

◄ Write at least ten descriptive sentences and make an accurate sketch of one or more objects on the next page.

Journal Entry

Location: _____

Date: _____

Time: _____

Observations: _____

_____

_____

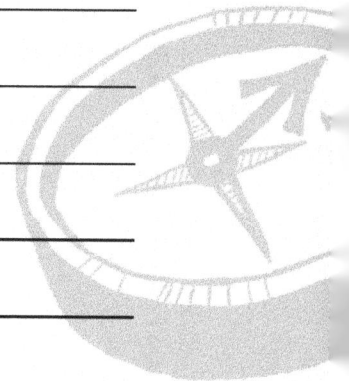

More observations: _____

_____

_____

_____

Sketches:

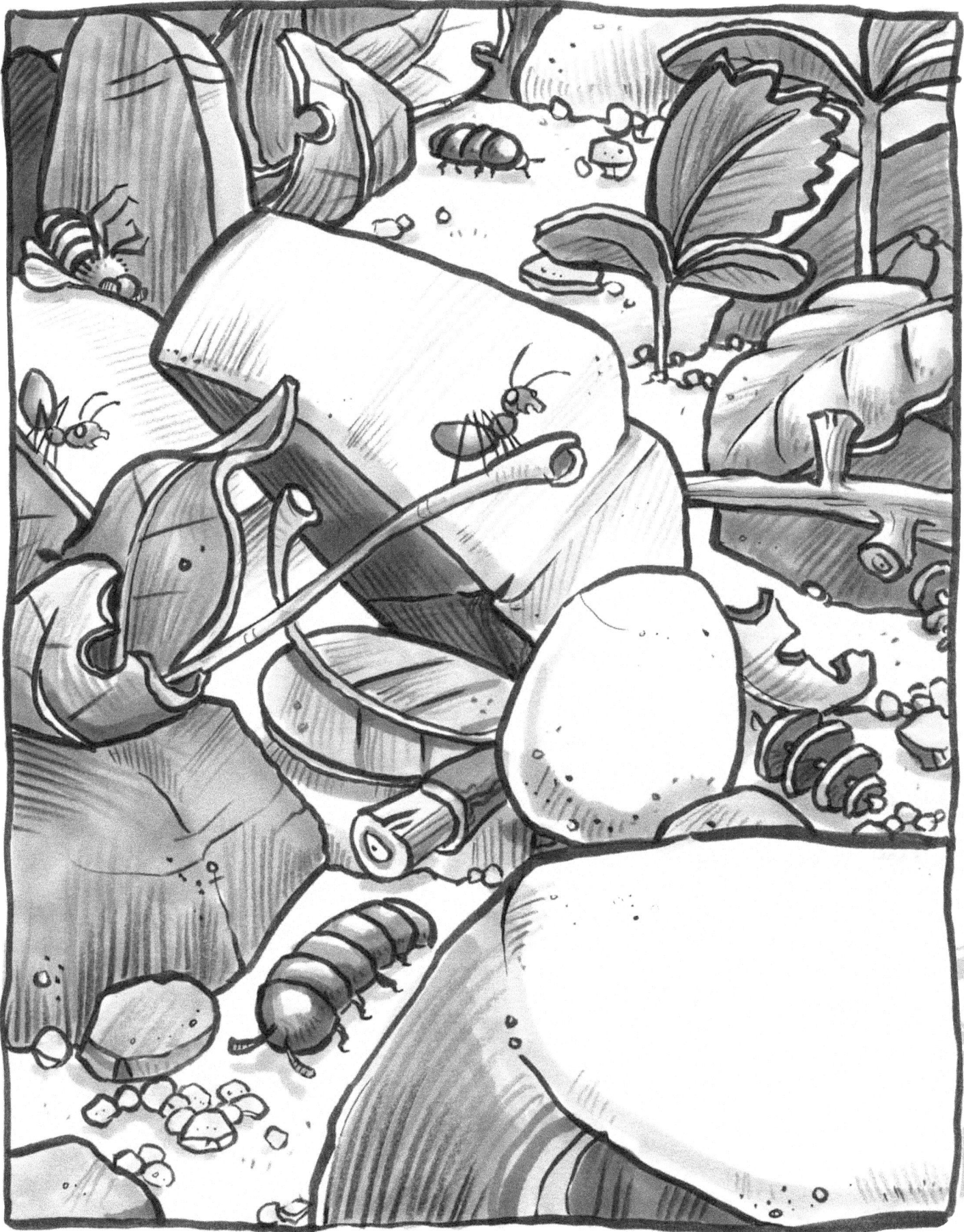

Sense Safaris: Touch Safari

Background: Discover your backyard by using all of your senses. You will appreciate your backyard in unique ways after this investigation.

Directions: Have a parent or friend collect four natural objects. Without looking, carefully feel the objects individually and write down your descriptions of each object in the chart to the right. Next, look at each object and add a "sighted" description. Then answer the questions below.

Respond to the following:

☝ Describe how feeling an object without looking at it was different from feeling it while looking at it. _____

_____

☝ Was there an object that startled you, either before you saw it or afterward? Explain. _____

_____

Object #1	Description without looking: _____ _____ _____ Description using your sight: _____ _____ _____
Object #2	Description without looking: _____ _____ _____ Description using your sight: _____ _____ _____
Object #3	Description without looking: _____ _____ _____ Description using your sight: _____ _____ _____
Object #4	Description without looking: _____ _____ _____ Description using your sight: _____ _____ _____

Follow the Beat of the Drum

Background: Have you ever gone the same route to school and then suddenly seen something you had never seen before, something you just had missed? By wearing shoes we actually do this to our sense of touch. Our protective shoes partially cut us off from our environment.

Directions: Do this fun activity with friends and family in a natural, safe area. It can be an amazing experience.

- Assign one person to be a drummer.

- Direct this person to stand off in the distance and beat a drum at regular intervals.

- Everyone else should become explorers.

- The explorers must take off their shoes and walk blindfolded.

- Slowly and carefully, the explorers should walk toward the sound of the drum, cautiously feeling their way with their bare feet. As they walk, the explorers should think about the feel of the land.

- When the explorers reach the drummer and tag him, they should take off their blindfolds and spend two to three minutes thinking about the "blind" journey they have just undertaken.

- The explorers should then return to the starting point, put on their shoes, and repeat the original walk with their eyes wide open. Finally, the explorers should write a diamonte poem comparing the two journey experiences. The directions are on the next page.

Structure of a Diamonte Poem:

Title

Line 1	First Walk
Line 2	Two adverbs describing the first walk
Line 3	Three adjectives describing the first walk
Line 4	Four "ing" words describing the first walk
Line 5	Five- to seven-word phrase connecting the first and second walks
Line 6	Four "ing" words describing the second walk
Line 7	Three adjectives describing the second walk
Line 8	Two adverbs describing the second walk
Line 9	Second Walk

Write the poem in Word or Pages and lay it out in a diamond shape. Decorate it creatively using natural objects you have collected, clip art, or original artwork.

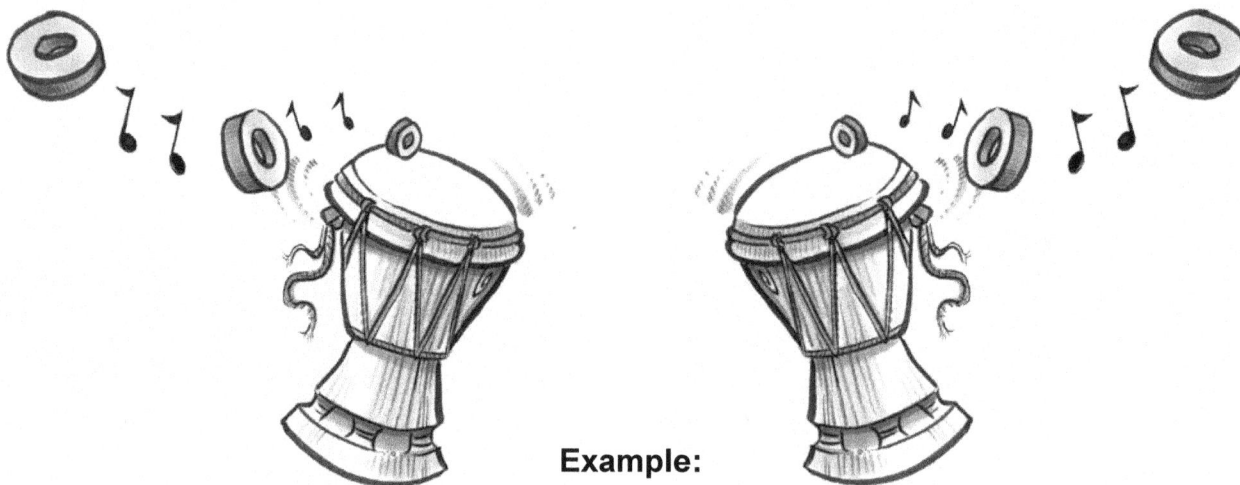

Example:

First Walk
Awkwardly, blindly
tangy, dusty, strange
Stumbling, groping, sloping, inching
Moving in stops and starts till sunlight filtered in
Marching, seeing, following, knowing
Sparkling, bright, familiar
Confidently, quickly
Second Walk

activity

Bio Bingo

Background: Everyone loves a good bingo game. This game challenges your outdoor skills. Use a small pencil instead of bingo chips to keep track of your findings.

Directions: Take the Bingo sheets provided and try to find the natural items listed as you explore the outdoors. Play regular bingo, finding five items in any straight line. Eventually, you can graduate to playing "around the world," crossing out all perimeter squares, or "black out," where all squares are crossed out. Use your pencil lightly so you can play with the same card many times. Enjoy looking carefully and respectfully for each natural item.

Card 1

Cumulus (Puffy) Cloud	Fly	White Flower	Spider Web	Hawk
Any Black-Colored Bird	Pill Bug	An Insect on a Leaf	A Singing Bird	Earthworm
Woodpecker	Spider	FREE SPACE	Dragonfly	Bee
Butterfly	Feather	Grass	Humming-bird	Lizard
Red Flower	Wild Animal Scat	Stratus (Blanket) Cloud	Evergreen Tree	Mushroom

Card 2

Grass	Pill Bug	Dragonfly	Purple Flower	Butterfly
Wild Animal Scat	Insect on a Leaf	Woodpecker	Fly	Stratus (Blanket) Cloud
Cumulus (Puffy) Cloud	Black-Colored Bird	FREE SPACE	Mushroom	Evergreen Tree
Lizard	White Flower	Singing Bird	Red Flower	Spider Web
Bee	Hawk	Humming-bird	Spider	Feather

Focus on: John Muir

It is no mistake that a silhouette of John Muir facing Half Dome in Yosemite Valley appears on the California State quarter. John Muir embodies all that is great about the wilderness areas in California. At the age of eleven, John and his Scottish family came to America to start a new life. At the age of thirty, John traveled to California and was introduced to the stunning Yosemite Valley. He instantly became enchanted by the grandeur of the Sierra Nevada Mountains, from the granite outcrops to the spring flowers. In Yosemite, he felt at home.

But, like many people who feel passionately about a special place, he was driven to preserve its beauty. People who had never seen Yosemite came to love it through the colorful and descriptive writings of John Muir. He even attracted the attention of the President of the United States, Teddy Roosevelt. President Roosevelt came to Yosemite in person to talk with John Muir and while there, discovered what was so special about the land. John and the president camped out together and shared their mutual respect and awe for wilderness. Two years later, John Muir was elated when Congress declared Yosemite Valley and the surrounding area a national park, preserving it for all of us to enjoy.

A Watershed Wander

Background: Water is essential for life, yet we often take for granted that we can turn on the tap and have fresh water at our fingertips. Throughout history, cultures have had to devise ingenious ways to move water across the landscape for farming and daily life.

Investigation: Do you know the origin of the water that flows out of your faucets?

1. Research where your water comes from. A good place to start is by investigating your local water district's Web site.

2. Research where the water goes after it spills into your drain. For most people in North America, it will lead to a water treatment plant. These plants often give fascinating free tours. How is your drain water cleaned, and where does it go next?

Activity: Pack a backpack with snacks, a camera or sketching supplies, and this workbook. You are going on a scouting expedition to find where the water that runs off your home goes. You will play the role of a travel journalist, recording the interesting details of your adventure.

Begin by looking at the roof of your house or the highest part of the land where your home is. Imagine that it is raining. Where exactly will the water run down to? Where do the gutters on the roof drain? When the water gets to a street, which way does the street gutter take it? When it goes underground, can you get enough of a peek to follow its general direction? Where does it go next? The idea is to follow this water as far as you possibly can and record what you discover along the way.

How far were you able to follow the water from your home? Draw some things you saw along the way: _____

_____

_____

_____

_____

Describe what you learned about the journey water takes after raining upon your house: _____

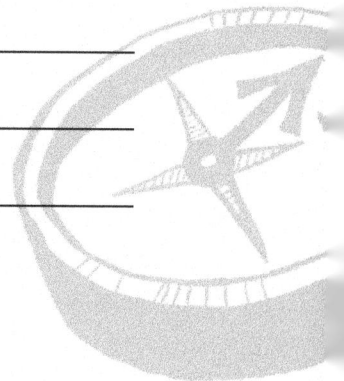

_____

_____

_____

Reflections: Eventually, if you walk far enough, you will come to a place where the man-made water channels meet natural ones. For example, a large metal pipe collecting water from the street gutters in a neighborhood may spill into the nearest creek. It is suggested that all water that doesn't evaporate on the way eventually finds its way to the ocean, although it may have to travel for hundreds of miles.

Do you think this is true of the water that rains on your rooftop or flows down your drain? Go to Google maps and trace how this might happen. Where would your water eventually enter the ocean if it could flow that far?

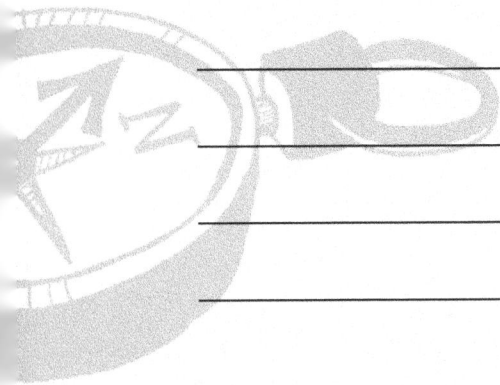

_____

_____

_____

_____

_____

Concerned Citizen: When we wash our cars or they leak oil, these oils and soaps eventually find their way to wild waterways. How might this affect plant and animals living there? _____

_____

_____

What could people do to lessen this impact?_____

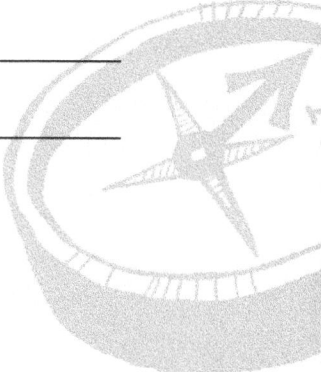

_____

_____

_____

_____

www.ingramcontent.com/pod-product-compliance
Lightning Source LLC
Chambersburg PA
CBHW042339030426
42335CB00030B/3408